Sea Horses

by Sally M. Walker

Lerner Publications Company • Minneapolis, Minnesota

Thanks to our series consultant, Sharyn Fenwick, elementary science and math specialist. Mrs. Fenwick was the winner of the National Science Teachers Association 1991 Distinguished Teaching Award. She also was the recipient of the Presidential Award for Excellence in Math and Science Teaching, representing the state of Minnesota at the elementary level in 1992.

The photographs in this book are reproduced with permission from: © Doug Perrine/ Seapics.com, pp. 4, 8, 15, 20, 27; © Rudie Kuiter/Seapics.com, pp. 5, 6, 10, 24, 33, 34, 35, 37; © David Kearnes/Seapics.com, pp. 7, 13, 41; © John G. Shedd Aquarium/Edward G. Lines Jr./Seapics.com, pp. 9, 12, 16, 39, 46-47; © Franco Banfi/Seapics.com, p. 11; © Kjell B. Sandved/Visuals Unlimited, pp. 14, 26, 38; © Clay Bryce/Seapics.com, p. 17; © Ingrid Visser/Seapics.com, p. 18 (inset); © M. Stack/Tom Stack & Associates, p. 18; © Mark Conlin/Seapics.com, pp. 19, 32; © Tom Stack/Tom Stack & Associates, p. 21; © Mako Hirose/Seapics.com, p. 22; © Therisa Stack/Tom Stack & Associates, p. 23; © Tom and Therisa Stack/Tom Stack & Associates, p. 25; © Jon Bertsch/Visuals Unlimited, p. 28; © Brandon D. Cole/Visuals Unlimited, p. 29; © Christopher Crowles/Visuals Unlimited, p. 30; © Marc Bernardi/Seapics.com, pp. 30 (inset), 31; © Randy Morse/Seapics.com, p. 36; © Rick Poley/ Visuals Unlimited, p. 40; © Tomas Bertelsen/The Rolex Awards for Enterprise, p. 42; © Mark Strickland/Seapics.com, p. 43. Cover photograph © John G. Shedd Aquarium/Edward G. Lines Jr./Seapics.com.

Text copyright © 2004 by Sally M. Walker

Lerner Publications Company
A division of Lerner Publishing Group
241 First Avenue North
Minneapolis, MN 55401 U.S.A.

Website address: www.lernerbooks.com

Library of Congress Cataloging-in-Publication Data

Walker, Sally M.
    Sea horses / by Sally M. Walker.
      p. cm. — (Early bird nature books)
    Includes index.
    Summary: An introduction to the physical characteristics,
  behavior, habitats, and life cycle of sea horses.
      ISBN 0–8225–3051–1 (lib. bdg. : alk. paper)
      1. Sea horses—Juvenile literature. [1. Sea horses.] I. Title.
  II. Series.
  QL638.S9 W35 2004
  597'.6798—dc21   2002014357

Manufactured in the United States of America
1 2 3 4 5 6 – JR – 09 08 07 06 05 04

Contents

Be a Word Detective

Can you find these words as you read about the sea horse's life? Be a detective and try to figure out what they mean. You can turn to the glossary on page 46 for help.

brood pouch   **gills**   **oxygen**

camouflage   **habitats**   **predators**

coral reefs   **holdfast**   **prey**

fins   **home range**

Chapter 1

This animal is a sea horse. Where do sea horses live?

What Is a Sea Horse?

A face like a horse's peeks around a rock. A tail like a monkey's grips a plant stem. This animal does not live on land, like horses and monkeys do. It is a fish. It lives underwater!

6

This strange fish is called a sea horse. Some species, or kinds, of sea horses are smaller than the tip of your little finger. The largest species are longer than your foot.

There are about 32 sea horse species. The tiny sea horses in this picture are smaller than a person's fingertip.

Sea horses are different from most other fish in many ways. Most fish have scales. Scales are thin, hard plates that protect a fish's body. Sea horses do not have scales. But sea horses do have tough skin. It protects them from sharp rocks.

Tough skin protects a sea horse from cuts and scrapes.

Skin stretches tightly over a sea horse's bony rings. The rings make the sea horse's body look bumpy.

Most fish have a backbone and ribs that shape their body. Sea horses have a backbone, but no ribs. Instead, sea horses have many small bones that fit together to make rings. The rings go all the way down a sea horse's body and into its tail.

A sea horse can wrap its tail around any small object.

A sea horse's tail has so many bony rings that it bends easily. A sea horse's tail can wrap around objects just like a monkey's tail can. An object that a sea horse's tail wraps around is called a holdfast. A sea horse grabs the nearest holdfast whenever the water moves. The tail holds tight to keep the sea horse from floating away.

Fish swim with body parts called fins. Most fish have a strong tail fin. The tail fin pushes these fish through the water.

A shark swims with its strong tail fin. The tail fin moves from side to side to push the shark through the water.

A sea horse swims by waving the small, thin fin on its back. The sea horse sinks when this fin is not moving.

Sea horses cannot swim as fast as other kinds of fish. Sea horses have no tail fin at all. They swim with a small, thin fin on their back. This fin waves back and forth. The waving pushes the sea horse slowly through the water.

Sea horses also have a small fin on each side of their head. Sea horses steer with these fins. They help sea horses twist and turn easily.

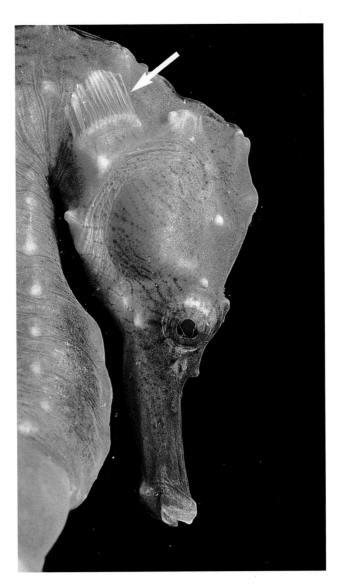

The fins on a sea horse's head are hard to see. The arrow in this picture is pointing to a head fin.

A sea horse usually swims with its head facing forward. The tail points downward. A sea horse can swim this way because it has a neck. The neck lets the sea horse bend its head. Most fish don't have a neck. They swim with their head pointing forward and their tail pointing backward.

A swimming sea horse can twist and turn to move between plants and rocks. It can even turn around in circles as it swims up or down.

14

Gills are found inside tiny slits on a fish's head. Most fish have gills shaped like hair combs. But a sea horse's gills are shaped like grapes. The gills are too small for a person to see.

Sea horses have another body part that helps them live underwater. Most creatures need a gas called oxygen (AHK-sih-juhn) to live. Oxygen is found in air and in water. Animals get oxygen by breathing. Sea horses and other fish use body parts called gills to breathe underwater. A sea horse's gills are inside slits on the sides of its head. Water flows into the slits. The gills remove oxygen from the water.

15

Chapter 2

These sea horses live among grassy plants. Why does grass make a good home for sea horses?

Sea Horse Homes

Sea horses live mainly in three kinds of homes. These homes are called habitats (HAB-uh-tats). A habitat is an area where a kind of animal can live and grow. All three sea horse habitats are found in warm ocean water that is not very deep.

Many sea horses live in sea grass beds.
These thick patches of sea grass grow underwater.
They look like underwater meadows. Blades of
sea grass make good holdfasts for sea horses.

Many small underwater animals live in sea grass beds. Blades of sea grass give these animals safe places to hide from hunting fish.

Mangrove trees grow tall above the water (above). *But their roots grow underwater, into the ocean floor* (inset).

Sea horses also live around the roots of mangrove trees. Mangrove trees grow in shallow ocean water. Their trunks and leaves grow above the water. Their long, twisty roots grow into the ocean floor. A sea horse's tail can easily hold on to mangrove roots.

This colorful coral reef is home to many fish. Groups of corals can be shaped like fans, branches, or other objects.

Coral reefs are the third sea horse habitat. Corals are tiny sea animals that live in groups. Corals have hard skeletons outside their bodies. Together, many coral skeletons form rocky mounds called reefs. Coral reefs have many small branches that sea horses' tails can grab.

This sea horse may stay in the same place for many hours. If it decides to move, it will not travel far.

A sea horse does not move around much in its habitat. It stays in one small area. This area is the sea horse's home range. Male sea horses live in a home range that is about the size of a card table. A female's home range is the size of half of a tennis court.

Many kinds of fish live in schools. Schools are groups of fish who swim together. Sea horses do not live in schools. Sea horses live alone most of the time.

These snappers swim together in a school for safety. An attacking fish would not be able to catch all of the snappers in the school.

Chapter 3

This sea horse lives alone on an old fishing net. Who does a female sea horse visit each morning?

A Sea Horse's Day

Most sea horses form pairs when they become adults. Each pair has one female and one male. These pairs do not live together. But they visit each other every morning. A female sea horse swims through her home range to her partner's home range.

Sea horses are usually brown or black. But they can change colors. Sea horse pairs change to a brighter color when they meet.

Two partners share a morning visit. Many sea horses keep the same partner for their whole life.

The two sea horses swim together for a few minutes. Sometimes they join tails. Then their colors return to normal. The female swims away. She will come back for another visit the next day.

Sea horse partners visit for about 10 minutes each day.

Scientists think that sea horses see very well. No one knows if sea horses can hear or smell.

The rest of a sea horse's day is usually spent in one place. The sea horse hangs on to a holdfast. It watches for prey. Prey are the animals sea horses hunt and eat. Sea horses are good watchers. They can move each eye in a different direction. One eye can look up while the other looks down.

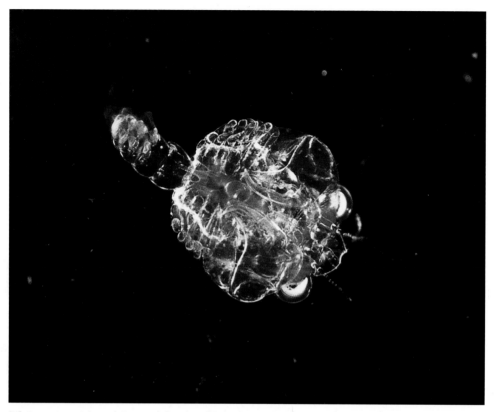

This sea animal is much smaller than it looks in this picture. It is about the size of an apple seed. Tiny sea animals make good meals for sea horses.

The moving eyes watch for tiny sea animals such as baby fish or shrimp. These animals are the sea horse's prey. The sea horse's head darts forward when prey swims near. The long snout works like a vacuum cleaner. It quickly sucks in the prey.

Sea horses also watch for predators (PREH-duh-turz). Predators are animals that hunt and eat other animals. Crabs, rays, sharks, and some birds eat adult sea horses. Many kinds of fish eat baby sea horses.

This animal is a called a leopard ray because it has spots like a leopard's. Rays hunt and eat sea horses.

This sea horse is trying to blend in with the coral branches around it.

Sea horses are not good fighters. They must hide from predators. To hide, sea horses try to blend in with the things around them. This way of hiding is called camouflage (KAM-uh-flahzh).

A hiding sea horse stays very still. It tries to look like a plant or a branch of coral. It changes color to match the rocks or plants nearby. Then predators can't see the sea horse.

Changing color helps a sea horse hide. Even the outer part of a sea horse's eye can change color.

Sea horses use both their shape (above) *and their color* (inset) *to hide.*

Some species of sea horses have spikes of skin on their head and back. The spikes look like plant stems or coral branches. These sea horses blend in even better with the plants around them.

This sea horse has round bumps on its skin. The bumps look like parts of the coral the sea horse is hiding on.

Chapter 4

These two sea horses are babies. Who gives birth to baby sea horses?

Parents and Babies

Most kinds of fish start out as eggs inside their mother's body. Sea horses do, too. Some mother fish lay their eggs in the water. Others give birth to live babies. But sea horses are not born from their mothers at all. They are born from their fathers!

How do sea horse eggs move from the mother's body to the father's? The mother sea horse visits the father every day. One day, she puts her eggs into the father's brood pouch. The brood pouch is a pocket on the male sea horse's belly. Eggs can grow safely there.

The sea horse on the right is a father with a brood pouch full of eggs. The sea horse on the left is the mother who put the eggs in the father's brood pouch.

One sea horse father gave birth to 1,572 babies at one time. Scientists counted every single baby!

The father's belly gets fatter as the baby sea horses grow. The pouch opens when the babies are ready to be born. The father bends and twists his body to help them come out. The babies swim out of the pouch. Some species of sea horses have about 12 babies at a time. Other species have about 100 to 200 babies.

Sea horses are on their own as soon as they are born. They look for a holdfast right away. A sea horse without a holdfast may be swept away by rushing water. Next, the babies look for food. Each baby must eat thousands of tiny sea animals every day to stay alive.

Newborn sea horses are about as long as a person's little fingernail. They are as thin as a piece of thread.

This mat of seaweed has holdfasts, hiding places, and prey for baby sea horses.

Young sea horses must also hide from predators. The babies often hide in mats of floating seaweed. The seaweed has good holdfasts. Other baby animals hide in seaweed, too. They make fine meals for the baby sea horses.

Sea horses grow quickly. They are fully grown when they are six months to one year old.

A young sea horse slurps up a meal. Small sea horse species live about one year. Larger species may live four years or more.

Chapter 5

These sea horses have been killed and dried to be used as medicine for people. How else do people harm sea horses?

Sea Horses and People

People do not eat sea horses. But we harm sea horses in many ways. Some people make medicine from dead sea horses. Craft makers use dried sea horses for key rings, paperweights, and pins.

Some people keep sea horses as pets, too. But most pet sea horses die quickly. Their owners do not always feed them the right foods. Sea horses also get sick easily. Their diseases are hard to cure.

These sea horses live in an aquarium run by experts. It is hard for people who are not experts to keep pet sea horses healthy.

Machines dig up the ocean floor to make room for big ships to sail through. This kind of digging destroys sea horse habitats.

Sea horse habitats are also in danger. Some builders drain the water from sea grass beds and mangrove swamps. The builders put up houses on the dry land that is left behind. Other people dig up and grind coral reefs to make concrete for sidewalks. Draining and digging destroy sea horse homes.

How can we help sea horses? We can use medicines made without sea horses. We can stop buying crafts made from dead sea horses. We can stop buying sea horses as pets. We can pass laws to protect sea horses' homes.

This sea horse belongs to a species that lives near South Africa. The species may die out forever because its habitat has been destroyed by people.

Sea horses are protected in these waters near the Philippine Islands in Southeast Asia. Guards watch from the building to make sure no one fishes here.

People have already helped sea horses by making ocean parks where fishing is not allowed. All of the fish that live in these parks are safe.

We are learning to take better care of sea horses and their homes. That way, sea horses will live in the oceans for many years to come.

The colorful sea horse is an amazing animal. People will keep working to help sea horses stay alive in Earth's oceans.

On Sharing a Book

As you know, adults greatly influence a child's attitude toward reading. When a child sees you read, or when you share a book with a child, you're sending a message that reading is important. Show the child that reading a book together is important to you. Find a comfortable, quiet place. Turn off the television and limit other distractions, such as telephone calls.

Be prepared to start slowly. Take turns reading parts of this book. Stop and talk about what you're reading. Talk about the photographs. You may find that much of the shared time is spent discussing just a few pages. This discussion time is valuable for both of you, so don't move through the book too quickly. If the child begins to lose interest, stop reading. Continue sharing the book at another time. When you do pick up the book again, be sure to revisit the parts you have already read. Most importantly, enjoy the book!

Be a Vocabulary Detective

You will find a word list on page 5. Words selected for this list are important to the understanding of the topic of this book. Encourage the child to be a word detective and search for the words as you read the book together. Talk about what the words mean and how they are used in the sentence. Do any of these words have more than one meaning? You will find these words defined in a glossary on page 46.

What about Questions?

Use questions to make sure the child understands the information in this book. Here are some suggestions:

> What did this paragraph tell us? What does this picture show? What do you think we'll learn about next? Where do sea horses live? Could a sea horse live near you? Why or why not? What can a sea horse's tail do? How do sea horses hide? Why do they hide? How are sea horses like other kinds of fish? How are they different? Who gives birth to sea horse babies? How are sea horse babies born? What is your favorite part of the book? Why?

If the child has questions, don't hesitate to respond with questions of your own, such as: What do *you* think? Why? What is it that you don't know? If the child can't remember certain facts, turn to the index.

Introducing the Index

The index is an important learning tool. It helps readers get information quickly without searching throughout the whole book. Turn to the index on page 47. Choose an entry, such as *eating*, and ask the child to use the index to find out what sea horses eat. Repeat this exercise with as many entries as you like. Ask the child to point out the differences between an index and a glossary. (The index helps readers find information quickly, while the glossary tells readers what words mean.)

Where in the World?

Many plants and animals found in the Early Bird Nature Books series live in parts of the world other than the United States. Encourage the child to find the places mentioned in this book on a world map or globe. Take time to talk about climate, terrain, and how you might live in such places.

All the World in Metric!

Although our monetary system is in metric units (based on multiples of 10), the United States is one of the few countries in the world that does not use the metric system of measurement. Here are some conversion activities you and the child can do using a calculator:

WHEN YOU KNOW:	MULTIPLY BY:	TO FIND:
miles	1.609	kilometers
feet	0.3048	meters
inches	2.54	centimeters
gallons	3.787	liters
tons	0.907	metric tons
pounds	0.454	kilograms

Activities

Pretend you are a sea horse hiding from a predator. Can you wear colors to help you blend in with the things around you? Can you stay very still? What else can you do to hide the way a sea horse does?

Pretend your finger is a sea horse's tail. What objects can you grip with your pretend tail? Would these objects make a good holdfast for a sea horse? Why or why not?

Glossary

brood pouch: a pocket on the belly of a male sea horse. Babies grow in the brood pouch before they are born.

camouflage (KAM-uh-flahzh): hiding by trying to look like nearby objects

coral reefs: mounds of rock made by tiny sea animals called corals

fins: body parts that fish use to swim and steer

gills: body parts that fish use to breathe

habitats (HAB-uh-tats): areas where a kind of animal can live and grow

holdfast: an object a sea horse holds onto with its tail

home range: a small area where a sea horse lives

oxygen (AHK-sih-juhn): a gas most creatures need to live

predators (PREH-duh-turz): animals that hunt and eat other animals

prey: animals that are hunted and eaten by other animals

Index

Pages listed in **bold** type refer to photographs.

About the Author

Sally M. Walker has written many books for young readers, including *Fireflies* in the Early Bird Nature series and the early reader *Mary Anning: Fossil Hunter*. She also coauthored the Early Bird Physics series with Roseann Feldmann. When she isn't busy writing and researching her books, Ms. Walker works as a children's literature consultant. She has taught children's literature at Northern Illinois University and has given presentations at many reading conferences. While she writes, Ms. Walker shares desk space with her family's two cats, who often jump onto the keyboard as she types. Ms. Walker lives in Illinois with her husband and two children.